Getting a Grip on ADD:

A Kid's Guide to Understanding and Coping with Attention Disorders

by

Kim "Tip" Frank, Ed.S., LPC
Counselor/Psychotherapist
Rock Hill School District
Carmel Counseling & Pyschological Services
Rock Hill, SC

Susan J. Smith, Ed.D.
School of Education
Winthrop University
Rock Hill, SC

Illustrated by Jan Hanna Elliott

Copyright 1994

Educational Media Corporation®
P.O. Box 21311
Minneapolis, MN 55421-0311

(612) 781-0088

ISBN 0-932796-60-5

Library of Congress Catalog No. 94-070341

Printing (Last Digit)

9   8   7   6   5   4   3

Production editor—

    Don L. Sorenson, Ph.D.

Graphic Design—

    Earl Sorenson

Special thanks...

A special thanks to Dr. Jan Shaw, Dr. Mitsuko Shannon, and Dr. Patricia Tonkowicz for the direction and support that they provided in the writing of this book.

Note to parents and health professionals:

This book is intended to aid children in dealing with attention disorders. The book was carefully written to be user friendly for children. We trust that the vocabulary, illustrations, and limited number of words on each page will make this book inviting and helpful to children in their understanding of Attention Deficit Disorder (ADD) and Attention Deficit Hyperactivity Disorder (ADHD).

The second part of this book focuses on practical ideas children can use to better cope in and outside of school. We believe in each child's ability to work out problems in his or her own life. This section is interactive in nature. The student selects areas of concern and does activities which will help him or her to explore what needs to be done to improve. In essence, self-improvement projects are provided that are creative, fun, and practical.

While the book can be used independently by elementary and middle school students, we highly recommend that parents and mental health professionals read and discuss this book with the children. In this way the information and suggestions are fully discussed and the children are encouraged to follow through on the coping strategies that are provided. Best wishes as you put this book to good use!

Kim "Tip" Frank, Ed.S., LPC
Susan J. Smith, Ed.D.

Table of Contents

Part I

Helping Children Understand Attention Disorders

Going to school is something every child must do. It can be hard work to listen all day and to do well in all of your subjects.

We learn by taking in information through our senses and sending this information to our brain.

We learn by seeing, hearing, touching, smelling, and tasting. All of these senses send thousands of signals to our brain every day.

In school it is important to be able to decide what is most necessary to be heard and seen in order for us to do well. We must learn how to sort all of the messages we receive into those we need and those we don't need.

For example, we need to hear the teacher's directions and to write our assignments down that are written on the blackboard. We don't need to hear a friend tapping a pencil on the desk or see the janitor picking up trash outside.

By paying close attention to those messages we need, we can usually follow directions well in school and therefore become better students.

Some students have a hard time tuning out distractions. They pay attention to noises and messages they don't need. These students become frustrated and confused because they have difficulty paying attention and focusing on the information which is most important.

Kim "Tip" Frank, Ed.S., LPC and Susan J. Smith, Ed.D.

In school it is hard to pay attention all of the time. We all daydream or feel restless sometimes. However, if you have trouble paying attention often and this has been going on for a long time, you may have a problem and need assistance.

We call this problem an attention disorder. You, and many others like you, may have trouble staying attentive. You have a shortage—or a deficit—of attention-holding ability. You simply have trouble paying attention or you can't seem to finish your work.

If we use the first letter of each of the words used to describe the problem, we call this problem:

ADD—   Attention Deficit Disorder

If you are always on the "go" and have lots of trouble sitting still, you may be hyperactive. This is where the H comes in the name ADHD—Attention Deficit Hyperactivity Disorder.

Students with ADD or ADHD say that they have some of these problems:

1. *Paying attention at school.*
2. *Keeping track of school work and responsibilities.*
3. *Making and keeping friends.*
4. *Being patient with others.*
5. *Knowing when to be quiet in class.*
6. *Staying out of fights.*
7. *Finishing classwork and homework.*
8. *Staying out of trouble and getting along with others.*

If you are one of these children, you are not alone. Teachers say that usually one or two students in every class have either ADD or ADHD.

It is important to know that students with ADD or ADHD are smart and healthy. However, a part of your brain used for concentration and controlling yourself may be a little low in certain chemical substances and it needs to be strengthened. In other words, part of your brain may be a little slow to react and it needs to be speeded up.

Kim "Tip" Frank, Ed.S., LPC and Susan J. Smith, Ed.D.

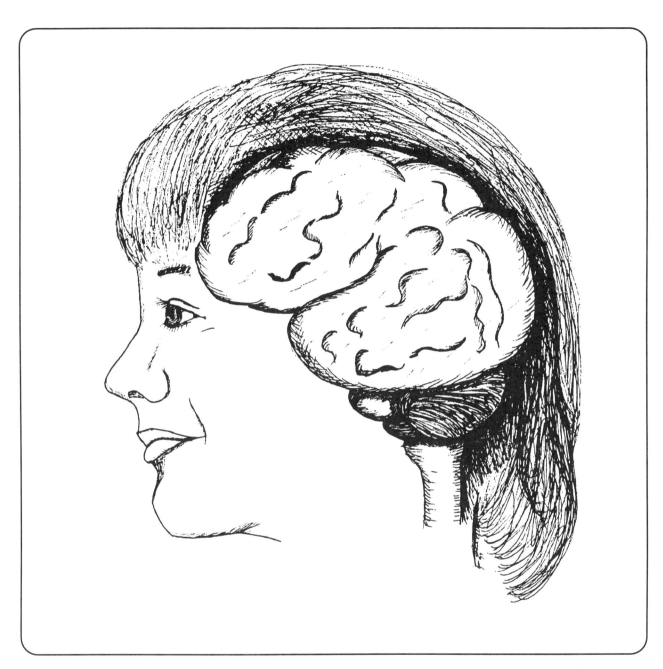

The part of your brain called the subcortex controls your ability to pay attention. It takes in messages from your senses of seeing, hearing, touching, smelling, and tasting. This section of the brain then must decide what you should pay attention to.

The subcortex has information dispatchers or runners made up of chemicals which carry messages. Many scientists think these chemical messengers may not be working quickly enough. Therefore, children with ADD or ADHD get confused when their senses take in so many messages at once that they can't pass along the most important information fast enough. It is like juggling many balls and not being able to keep up.

Kim "Tip" Frank, Ed.S., LPC and Susan J. Smith, Ed.D.

Sometimes it is helpful to speed up this area of the brain so you can draw a curtain across sights and noises that you don't need. Then you can focus harder on directions given by your teachers, parents, and friends and concentrate more on the work that you need to do.

One way that many doctors have helped ADD or ADHD students is to prescribe medication. This medication can replace some substances in your brain that are low and can help your brain to work faster. In this way you can pay better attention and ignore unimportant sights and sounds. You can also control yourself better with medication. You can think of medication for ADD or ADHD as being like a "fuel for the brain"—giving your brain more energy.

Kim "Tip" Frank, Ed.S., LPC and Susan J. Smith, Ed.D.

If your doctor has prescribed medication for you, it is important for you to notice your own feelings and behaviors so you can help your doctor and parents decide whether the medication helps you. Most students—in fact three out of every four students with ADD or ADHD taking medication—are helped greatly by taking the medication as prescribed by their doctor.

The medication most often given to children with ADD or ADHD is Ritalin®. Usually you take a pill in the morning at breakfast and one at lunch. Sometimes students take a pill again after school when it is time to do your homework. This is a decision your doctor will help you make.

Ritalin® is a registered trademark of Ciba Pharmaceuticals for methylphenidate.

Kim "Tip" Frank, Ed.S., LPC and Susan J. Smith, Ed.D.

Here are some comments students have made about taking medication to help them concentrate and control their behavior:

"I can think better."

"I don't get my name on the board very often anymore."

"It helps me to be more patient at home and school."

"It helps me to know when to walk away from trouble."

"I can really hear my teacher give directions now."

"I am now better able to think before I do things."

"I don't feel as tired."

"I am not in a bad mood as often."

Sometimes medication has what we call side effects. These are things that may happen that people don't like about medicine. Examples might be:

You may not feel as hungry at meal time.

You may get a slight stomachache when you take the pill. (If so, drinking a glass of water or juice and eating a snack usually helps.)

You may not sleep as well. (However, some say they sleep better.)

You may sweat more.

You may be more irritable at times. (In other words, you may feel a little more grumpy or moody.)

Kim "Tip" Frank, Ed.S., LPC and Susan J. Smith, Ed.D.

Usually if you do have any side effects, they go away within two weeks. Talk to your parents and doctor about how your body feels so they can help you. You should only take the number of pills your doctor prescribes.

Children with ADD or ADHD have feelings that need to be understood.

Some children say they are:

Unpopular   *Up and Down*

Frustrated

Tired   Picked on

Hyper

Jumpy   Confused

Worried

Impatient   **Grumpy**

Disorganized

It is good to know or recognize your different feelings and talk about them with your parents, teachers, counselors, doctors, and friends. This support will help you to make the decisions that are best for you.

Remember that there is no magic pill that will take away your problems. You must learn to be patient with yourself and to take responsibility for making decisions that are good for you. Having ADD or ADHD is not an excuse for misbehaving or not completing assignments.

The medication will likely help you, but you must help yourself most of all. You have the ability to work out the problems in your life.

*Whether you use medication or not, it is important to ask yourself the question, "What am **I** going to do about it?" Countless other children have learned to deal with their attention problem and be successful at school. You can, too!*

Part II

Practical Ideas to Cope with Attention Disorders

Following are some of the general concerns of most children with ADD/ADHD. Think about which ones you may need to improve and turn to the pages that are shown for some helpful ideas.

Self-Improvement Projects

1. Improving my study skills
   (learning how to study and getting more organized
   to improve my grades)   *Turn to page 37*

2. Listening and getting more out of each lesson
   (learning how to concentrate)   *Turn to page 44*

3. Getting along in school and staying out of trouble
   (learning self-control and improving your behavior)   *Turn to page 48*

4. Feeling better about myself
   (learning to like myself and dealing with my feelings)   *Turn to page 51*

5. Developing friendships with others
   (learning to get along with others and making friends) *Turn to page 55*

On the pages which follow are some helpful ideas that you can use with the help of your parents and teachers to improve your self-esteem and school achievement.

Terms

ADD-	Attention Deficit Disorder
ADHD-	Attention Deficit Hyperactivity Disorder
Clear Messages-	thinking good thoughts about yourself
Compliment-	saying something nice to another person
Cope-	making the best of your situation
Counselor-	a person who listens and talks to people about their feelings
Distractible-	to have trouble paying attention
Hyperactive-	overactive behavior, always on the "go"
Impulsive-	to do something without thinking first
Inattention-	not paying attention
Irritable-	to get upset easily at others
Medication-	medicine used to treat a problem
Muddy Messages-	thinking bad or negative thoughts about yourself
Self-esteem-	how you feel about yourself
Side Effects-	things that may happen that you don't like about medicine
Study Skills-	learning ways to be better organized in school
Support System-	people you know you can turn to for help
Time Management-	using your time wisely in order to get things done on time

Kim "Tip" Frank, Ed.S., LPC and Susan J. Smith, Ed.D.

1. Study Skills—Knowing How to Study

A. Study Tips

Knowing how to study is half the battle. You may be trying hard now, but the trick is studying *smarter*. Here are some study tips. Circle the ones you think you may need to work on.

1. Organization

a. Be prepared! Have a place for your materials so that you always know where they are. Before class make sure you have all materials needed (books, homework, pencils, pens, notebook, paper, special materials such as ruler, glue, markers, crayons, etc.). It is a good idea to use a three-ring notebook with dividers for each subject. You may want to highlight each section with a different color. Have plenty of paper available for each section to take notes and to keep homework assignments where they won't get lost.

b. Organize your desk! Each time you put something in it, know exactly where it goes. Avoid "stuffing." Start today by having a complete clean-out and fix-up. Put your books and notebooks in the same order each day so that you can find them without even looking.

c. If you have a locker, put your books sideways in the order that you will need them each day. Some stores even sell plastic shelves you can put in your locker to stay better organized.

d. Directions are important! Take the time to really read and understand each direction even if you think you know what to do.

e. Proofread your work! Check over it, see if it makes sense. Look for careless mistakes before handing in each assignment or test. We all make mistakes.

2. Listening

    a. Listen with your whole body! Look at the person who is talking. Turn your body toward the speaker; watch that person speaking. Keep your legs and hands still. Try to be interested in what the person is saying. This shows respect and helps you to learn more.

    b. Ask questions! Try to understand what the person is saying. When the person says something you do not understand, put your hand up and ask about it.

    c. Write it down! Write down anything you think is important. You may need to know it for an upcoming test or assignment.

    d. Concentrate! Think about what the person is saying. Put all other thoughts aside during the lesson.

    e. Listen to directions and write them down! Listen carefully to make sure you understand what to do.

    f. Keep a "to do" list as your teacher gives assignments and directions. Like with a grocery list, check each one off as they are completed.

              Kim "Tip" Frank, Ed.S., LPC and Susan J. Smith, Ed.D.

3. Homework

a. Schedule a time to study! Find out what time you study best and make that your regular study time.

b. Study where you can concentrate! Homework goes faster if there are no distractions around you such as a stereo, phone, television, other people, and so forth. It is best to try to find a regular study place that is quiet. You will need a good light, table, chair, and study materials.

c. Think before you leave school! Think of each subject and decide if you need to take anything home for that subject. An assignment notebook used for jotting things down during the day can help if you have trouble remembering, or use the Weekly School Schedule found in *Appendix A* or *Appendix D*-Homework Assignment Log. Many students use a folder with pouches. On the left side an assignment sheet (Appendix D) is kept for you to write down assignments. Completed assignments are kept on the right side. Keep your homework folder with you throughout each day. (Note how to color code your assignments in Appendix D. This makes for fun and good organization.)

d. Set a time limit to study! See how long you can concentrate. You might use a timer to set a time to really concentrate and then give yourself a break or a reward at the end of the time.

e. Have a special place for homework! When your homework is finished, put it in a special place and you will always have it ready to take to school. It is a good idea to keep it in your three-ring notebook in the section for whatever subject the assignment belongs.

4. Time Planning

a. Set goals for yourself! Decide what you have to do and how much time you have to spend doing it.

b. Do what is important first! If everything is important, it may be best to do the things that are the most unpleasant first, so that the worst will be out of the way.

c. Make each minute count! A few minutes of real concentration are worth more than hours of half attention.

d. Plan your day! The more organized you are, the less time you waste, and the more time you can schedule for things you like to do. (See *Appendix B* for a daily schedule.) You can plan out each day making sure you get your work done and still have time to do things you really want to do.

e. Reward yourself! When you are able to complete a goal, reward yourself with a few minutes of "free time," a star on your paper, a few minutes of daydreaming or something pleasant. Allow yourself to feel proud.

Having circled the ones that you think need improvement, try making a personal prescription.

Here is an example of a personal prescription to tape on the corner of your desk to help you monitor your progress.

Kim "Tip" Frank, Ed.S., LPC and Susan J. Smith, Ed.D.

Date: Tuesday, October 17   Name: Billy Bopper
1. Am I in my seat?
2. Do I have out the materials I need?
3. Am I talking to or touching anyone?
4. Am I listening to the teacher?
5. Did I write down my assignment for tomorrow?

Here is a blank prescription form for you to use. Choose some of the study tips you've circled and write them in the form of a question. It would be a good idea to let your teacher help you fill out your personal prescription.

Date: _____   Name: _____
1. _____
2. _____
3. _____
4. _____
5. _____

* Some students can be encouraged to fill out their own prescriptions. Make copies of the personal prescription form and use it daily.

B. Working With Your Teachers

Sometimes it helps to talk to your teacher to work out a plan to better cope (deal) with your Attention Deficit Disorder. Most teachers are very happy to work with students. Take a look at the suggestions for teachers that follow. These are called *accommodations*. An accommodation is when a teacher does something special to help you to learn better.

Accommodations

1. Change your seat to a quiet area. For example:
   a. Sit up front with your back to the rest of the class to keep other students out of view.
   b. Sit near the teacher's desk.
   c. Sit away from doors, windows, and air conditioners if possible.
   d. Sit near a serious student who works hard and doesn't bother others.
2. Request a "study buddy." (Sitting near a classmate who is a good student can help. This person can remind you to get back on task and can answer questions you may have.)
3. Request extra time to complete assigned work.
4. Teacher may shorten assignments. (Try to do more and more as you improve.)
5. Set a time limit for classwork to be done using a kitchen timer.
6. Have a private signal that your teacher can use to remind you to get back on task. (Example: A tap on the shoulder or a secret code word such as "BOT," which means get *Back on Task.*) See *Appendix C* "Signs" for more ideas of private signals you and your teacher may use.
7. Teacher asks student to repeat directions to make sure they are understood before beginning an activity or assignment.
8. Teacher regularly checks desk and notebook for neatness.
9. Teacher signs assignment pad at end of day to make sure assignments are written down correctly.
10. Other ideas.

If you believe any of these suggestions may help, put a check by the ones that you would like to discuss with your teacher. You and your teacher may come up with some others, also.

Kim "Tip" Frank, Ed.S., LPC and Susan J. Smith, Ed.D.

C. SQ3R

One way to learn faster and better is to use the following method or way of studying. When your teacher gives you something to read such as a science or social studies assignment, try the following:

Survey-   Quickly look over the assignment. Skim over the pages assigned and get an idea of what it is about. This should take less than a minute.

Question-   Look carefully at the questions at the end of the section which you will likely need to do for homework. Also look at the headings and try to turn them into questions.

Example: Heading-*School in Colonial Days*

Question-What was school like in Colonial Days?

Read-   Read to answer the questions. This is called *scanning.* This means you are just looking for the answers to questions and main ideas.

Write-   Take notes. Write down the answers to the questions and take a few notes on the main ideas.

Review-   Before you stop, take a minute to think about what you've learned. Look over your notes and quiz yourself.

2. Listening in Class and Concentrating

Paying attention in class is hard work but necessary in order to do a good job in school. Everyone catches themselves daydreaming during class at one time or another. Students with ADD can especially have trouble staying on task—or keeping your mind on what you are supposed to be doing. To help you understand what is needed to pay attention better, try the following trick.

A. Active Listening

Fold a dollar bill in an "S" shape and add two paper clips (one paper clip over two folds at each end). Pull the ends quickly in opposite directions and the clips join together in midair.

Notice how the paper clips seem to connect in midair. This is a picture of what you need to do to improve at school. You must connect with your teacher. There is a trick or listening skill you can use to connect or join together with your teacher. It is called active listening. Active listening has six simple steps that you can use during each lesson. (Adapted from Kim "Tip" Frank, Counseling *Props and Metaphors*, p. 15).

1. **Prepare–**   Prepare by starting to think about the lesson and putting aside whatever you are doing.

2. **Check–**   Check out or become aware of your feelings and thoughts that may interfere with the lesson. For example, you may be feeling hungry or angry. Possibly you are thinking about the game after school or some other activity.

3. **Block–**   Block out all thoughts and feelings for now in order to think about the lesson only. For example, if you are upset about something that happened earlier in the day, promise yourself that you will deal with that later.

4. **Promise–**   Promise yourself that you will do your best and really try to pay attention.

5. **Goal–**   Set a goal. Think about what exactly you can do to get the most out of the lesson. Here are some examples:

   a. Take notes writing down the most important ideas you want to remember.

   b. Participate at least two or three times during the lesson. Ask questions when you don't understand something and try to answer questions when you think you do know the answer.

   c. Try to listen so well that you can easily do the assignment after the lesson.

6. **Maintain–** Maintain your concentration and stay on task. Don't stop until the lesson is over. If you start to daydream, remember to BLOCK!

An easy way to remember these six steps is to memorize the following silly sentence. Each word stands for one of the six steps.

Peter Chased Bluish Purple Gooey Monsters.

Peter—	Prepare
Chased—	Check
Bluish—	Block
Purple—	Promise
Gooey—	Goal
Monsters—	Maintain

Memorize the six steps by using the silly sentence and Practice! Practice! Practice! When used with each lesson, active listening will become automatic. Then you will really connect with your teacher.

B. Beat the Clock

Another helpful way to concentrate and stay on task is to play a simple game. With each assignment (classwork or homework), try to guess how much time will be needed to finish it. At first you may need a teacher or parent to help you judge how much time the work will likely take. Now set a kitchen timer with the number of minutes you've guessed. If you have no kitchen timer, simply figure out on your watch or clock when you will need to finish. **Caution:** Please allow a little extra time so you *do not rush through the work.* As you work steadily, you'll find that you can beat the clock often. Better yet, you'll finish your work, and it won't take too long.

C. The Three C's for Success

By using the three exercises that follow, you will discover how to use three very important abilities you have. *The wooden toys used in exercises one and two can be obtained at the address that follows props one and two.* They are inexpensive and worth ordering because what is learned is long remembered.

Prop 1: Block and String

The block with string running through it moves easily downward as the string is relaxed. When the handles are pulled firmly, the block of wood, "Fred," stops immediately. "Fred's" downward movement is at your control according to how strongly you pull on the string handles.

By using "Fred," you have just discovered something very important. I want you to know that just as you controlled "Fred," you can control someone else. You guessed it, You! You can control yourself anytime you choose. If it helps, you can pretend that you have an invisible string inside of you called your self-control string. You can pull it anytime you need to control yourself.

[Adapted from Kim "Tip" Frank, *Counseling Props and Metaphors*, pp. 22-23.]

Prop 2: Flips or String Ball

Flip the ball into the air and attempt to make it go through the hole at the end of the wooden handle. This is easier said than done. The more you practice, the better you'll get.

This exercise is really a concentration test. Put your mind only on getting the ball through the hole and nothing else. Don't think about your friends or any problems you may have. Just think about doing this activity. *Ready, begin!*

This is called "blocking." In other words, we can learn to put other things out of our minds to finish the job at hand. Like with the flip game, with practice you can learn to concentrate in class by blocking. Remember, only think about one thing at a time.

To order these wooden toys write:

Carlisle of Newberry
E.B. "Ned" Carlisle
2105 Glenns St.
Newberry, SC 29108
(803) 276-3680

Prop 3: Following Directions Test

Do the following exercises and see if you can do them correctly. Be careful! You must follow the directions exactly. It will take some real thinking.

The Fun Test

Directions: Read carefully and follow all directions.

(A) Draw a big square to the right.
Put a circle in the top middle of the square.
Draw a small star to the right of the square.
Put a 7 in the center of the circle.
Draw a triangle under the circle.
Underline the number 7.

(B) Follow these directions carefully:

(1) Put an X on the first dot in row 3.

(2) Put an X on the fifth dot in row 3.

(3) Put an X on the first dot on row 7.

(4) Put an X on the fifth dot on row 7.

(5) Now join all the X's. What shape did you get?

```
1    .    .    .    .    .
2    .    .    .    .    .
3    .    .    .    .    .
4    .    .    .    .    .
5    .    .    .    .    .
6    .    .    .    .    .
7    .    .    .    .    .
8    .    .    .    .    .
```

*Now check your answer with the correct ones on page 49.

To follow directions and to do your work well involves really thinking. There's a funny word for thinking hard. It is called *cogitating.*

Therefore, the three C's for success that you need to remember and use are:

1. Self-Control-controlling yourself

2. Concentrate-thinking about only one thing, namely, what you are doing.

3. Cogitate-really using your brain to think hard. You have a good mind. Use it!

See if you can memorize the three words and what they mean. Write the three words down on a small index card and carry them with you as a reminder for success.

3. Behavior and Self-Control

If you have not read Section 2C "The Three C's for Success" (page 45), now would be a good time to read about self-control. Look at Prop 1: "Block and String." With practice you will learn that you, with the help of your medication, can control yourself. (See address on page 46.)

A. Using Your Head and Heart

One of the ways kids with ADD or ADHD get into trouble is by being *impulsive*. Impulsive means doing something without thinking. You need to give yourself permission to think before doing anything.

Perhaps your best two weapons against being impulsive are your head and heart. Your head, of course, involves using your brain power to make good decisions about how to act. Your heart is used to give you feelings about whether to do something or not. It is important to know how to listen to your feelings.

To use your *head*, always ask yourself these three questions before doing anything:

1. What am I getting ready to do?
2. What will happen if I do this?
3. What can I do instead?

Write these questions on a 3 X 5 inch index card or a small piece of paper. Carry it with you or tape it on your desk until you know them well. This card can be your "control card."

Using your heart means listening or "tuning in" to your feelings. Your feelings are important and shouldn't be ignored. Try this: Write down the following promise used in the Just Say No Club on another card or sheet of paper.

Just Say No Promise #4

"I promise, if I ever have a scared, uncomfortable feeling inside about doing something, I'll just say no."

When you have that Uh-oh feeling inside, your heart is telling you there is something wrong. Listen to your heart and think about doing the right thing.

Take the time to use your head and your heart. They are like two good friends. The split second it takes to think clearly and to notice your feelings will make the difference in getting along in school or not. It's up to you. You can control your behavior.

Kim "Tip" Frank, Ed.S., LPC and Susan J. Smith, Ed.D.

B. Charting

How will you know if you are improving? Charting means to keep track of your progress. You and your teacher can work together on this project.

Directions:

1. Talk to your teacher and set a goal. Choose one behavior which you both think you need to improve. (You can choose other behaviors to work on later. Just focus on the most important one for now.)

2. At the end of each day, briefly meet with your teacher and rate your behavior using the chart on page 50. Add up your points at the end of the week.

3. Agree upon a number of points you hope to earn by the end of the week to win a reward. Rewards may be extra play time, an ice cream coupon, being the teacher's helper, and so forth.

Behavior charting can be fun. It can help you to think more about your behavior and to make changes. Now, just do it!

Fun Test Answers

Activity A

Activity B

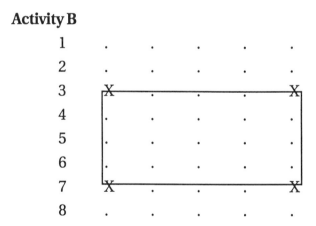

A rectangle

Sample Behavior Chart

Name _Sally Slider_

Behavior I'm trying to improve **staying in seat**

Number of points needed to earn reward __15__
A = 4; B = 3; C = 2; D = 1

Reward __helping P.E. teacher in morning__

Points Earned
Monday __4__ Tuesday __2__ Wednesday __3__ Thursday __3__ Friday __4__
Total for week __16__

Behavior Chart

Name _____

Behavior I'm trying to improve _____

Number of points needed to earn reward _____
A = 4; B = 3; C = 2; D = 1

Reward _____

Points Earned
Monday _____ Tuesday _____ Wednesday _____ Thursday _____ Friday _____
Total for week _____

Kim "Tip" Frank, Ed.S., LPC and Susan J. Smith, Ed.D.

4. Feeling Better About Myself

A. Clear Messages

I'm thinking of a person who is very important and special. This person is someone you see every day. This person is also one of the most important friends you could ever have. Can you name this person?

The answer is *YOU!* Sometimes we forget to be nice to ourselves and to learn to like ourselves. A lot of children with ADD or ADHD don't like themselves. They believe they are dumb or a nerd or something else. The truth is *all* children feel this way at one time or another. The key is not to keep feeling this way. This is called low *self-esteem.*

The best way to feel better about yourself is to change your way of thinking. Our thinking gets us into trouble. It can also get us out of trouble. You have basically two ways of thinking about yourself and the things that happen to you. We call them muddy messages and clear messages.

Muddy messages are thoughts that cause you to feel badly about yourself. You feel upset inside and things bother you.

Clear messages are just the opposite. Your thoughts make you feel good about yourself. You feel at peace inside and things don't bother you.

Here are some examples of clear versus muddy thinking.

Event	Muddy Message	Clear Message
Someone calls you a name.	"Everyone thinks I'm a jerk."	"People who call names are just trying to get others upset. I'm not going to pay attention to him."
You failed a test.	"What's the point in trying? I'll never pass this class. I'm dumb in math."	"I wish I would have done better. However, I'm still an O.K. person. I'll get some help and do better next time."

This is called *self-talk.* What you say to yourself makes all the difference. To feel good about yourself, it is important to think good thoughts. Good thoughts equal good feelings. Remember we all have things we're not really good at doing. It is okay not to be good at some things. What's important is to do your best and learn to like yourself.

One of the most important self-talk words to remember is *IALAC.* It stands for I Am Lovable and Capable. *Lovable* means people can love you just because of who you are. You are special not because of what you do but who you are. *Capable* means I can. You can do many things well. Take a minute to list at least two things you do well at school and outside of school.

In School	Out of School
1. _____	1. _____
2. _____	2. _____

On an index card, write the word IALAC. Let this be your secret code word. Take it with you to remind you that you are special and O.K.

IALAC is a wonderful clear message. There are many more that you can say to yourself. Try the following experiment this week. Every time something happens to you this week good or bad, give yourself a clear message. Catch your muddy messages and change them to clear messages. Remember, you control what you think. No junk thoughts! Practice using clear messages such as:

> "I'm O.K."

> "I can handle it."

> "I'll just do my best."

> "No one is perfect."

> "It's going to work out."

List some more clear messages you might give yourself.

1. _____

2. _____

3. _____

4. _____

5. _____

Kim "Tip" Frank, Ed.S., LPC and Susan J. Smith, Ed.D.

B. RAS Your Feelings

When it comes to feelings, we have all kinds. It is important to know how to handle feelings. The word RAS is another secret code word worth remembering. It reminds us of three important things to do with our feelings.

R stands for Recognize Your Feelings.

Recognize means to know or to think about your feelings. You have two types of feelings. Here are some examples under each type.

Pleasant Feelings		**Unpleasant Feelings**	
(Feelings we like to have)		(Feelings we don't like to have)	
happy	peaceful	sad	unhappy
excited	joyful	mad	worried
surprised	hopeful	upset	tired
warm		frustrated	stupid
proud		disappointed	nervous
delighted		left out	
love		scared	
friendly		guilty	
confident		embarrassed	
relaxed		jealous	

Recognizing or knowing what feelings you have is very important. Throughout each day, stop for a minute and listen to your feelings. Ask, how am I feeling right now? Your body and mind will tell you.

A stands for Accept Your Feelings.

Accept means that your feelings are always O.K. Accept means to take your feelings as they are. There is nothing wrong with feeling the way you do. Feelings are a part of you, and they are O.K.

S stands for Share Your Feelings.

Feelings are to be **shared** with others. Talking to people you trust about your feelings is a wonderful way to express your feelings. Feelings are not to be kept inside. You just feel better when you talk to others about your feelings. Who can you share your feelings with? Try to list at least three people whom you believe can be trusted with your deepest feelings.

People I Can Trust With My Feelings

1. _____

2. _____

3. _____

4. _____

5. _____

Basically, if you have some unpleasant feelings for more than a day or two, it is time to RAS your feelings. Remember, your feelings are always O.K. You do, however, need to recognize them and share them with people you trust such as your parents, teacher, or counselor.

5. Friendship: How to Make Friends

In math you've learned that 1 + 1 = 2. However, when it comes to friendship, 1 + 1 = 3. Think about it. If you know how to make one good friend, then you can make another. The trick is knowing how to make one good friend. Once you've learned that trick there is no limit to the number of friends you can make. So, 1 + 1 could equal 3 or 10 or 100 or who knows? Read over the next few pages to learn four simple steps you can use to develop friendships. It's called the "Friendship Model."

First be a good friend to yourself and then you are ready to be a good friend to others. One of the first friends you need to have is yourself. Learn to like yourself and think good thoughts about yourself.

It is important to have an idea of what a friend is like. What qualities or good things do you look for in a friend? List them below.

1. _____

2. _____

3. _____

4. _____

5. _____

Here are some ideas other students have shared:

> a good listener
>
> someone you trust
>
> patient
>
> flexible and doesn't get upset easily
>
> takes turns and shares
>
> kind and has good manners
>
> thinks before acting in a hurtful way

For some students, making friends and keeping friends seems to be easy. However, for many students who are shy, move a lot, or have an attention problem, the process can be frustrating.

In the "Friendship Model" there are four steps. The ***first step*** is to "Check Out" yourself and the kinds of messages you send to others. Are you sending clear messages or muddy messages?

Clear messages are positive messages such as looking at people, smiling, being polite, and helping others. Muddy messages are negative messages such as crying, whining, tattletaling, and pushing.

Make sure you send clear messages to others. You are then more likely to be the type of person others want to be around. Look for friends who also send clear messages back to you.

The ***second step*** is to "Reach Out." This is the step where you need to talk to others. If you don't know what to say, then you can give a compliment or you can use an everyday statement.

A compliment is when you say something nice to someone, such as:

"I like your T-shirt," or "You are a good ball player."

An everyday comment is a sentence about almost anything, such as:

"What is your favorite subject?," "Do you have any brothers or sisters?,"

"How old are you?," or "What movie is your all-time favorite?"

Can you make up a compliment? Write one or two for practice.

1. _____

2. _____

Can you make up an everyday statement? Write one or two for practice.

1. _____

2. _____

Kim "Tip" Frank, Ed.S., LPC and Susan J. Smith, Ed.D.

The *third step* is to "Try It Out."

When you go to the store to buy a pair of shoes, you try them on before you buy them. Well, the same thing goes with making friends. You should ask yourself whether these students are good for you as friends. Do you feel comfortable being with them? Step three involves deciding who your friends are going to be. Ask yourself about the friend or group, "Is it working?" and "Does it feel O.K.?"

If the answer is yes, then you move to *step four. "Work It Out."* This means to keep the friendship going. To keep friends you must work hard at being a friend yourself. Good friends usually share, are honest, are good listeners, and care about other people's feelings.

A good friend is not a jealous person. Try hard to be thoughtful and patient. Think before you say something that you might regret.

If your pals are not working out, then take a "Time Out" and ask yourself what is going wrong. Begin by checking yourself out again. Remember to send clear-not muddy-messages. Look for some other pals who send clear messages to you.

Try to remember the four-step friendship model. Think about each step every time you are trying to make and keep your friends. Note the following chart. The chart will help you to remember the four steps. You may want to talk to your school counselor and plan how you may use the four steps.

Friendship Model

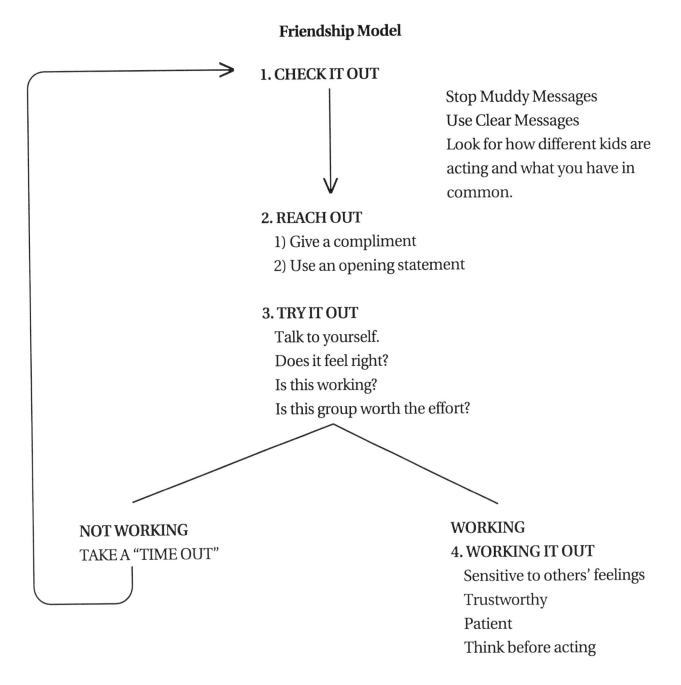

1. CHECK IT OUT

Stop Muddy Messages
Use Clear Messages
Look for how different kids are acting and what you have in common.

2. REACH OUT

1) Give a compliment
2) Use an opening statement

3. TRY IT OUT

Talk to yourself.
Does it feel right?
Is this working?
Is this group worth the effort?

NOT WORKING
TAKE A "TIME OUT"

WORKING
4. WORKING IT OUT
Sensitive to others' feelings
Trustworthy
Patient
Think before acting

Source: Smith, S.J. and Walter, G. Four Steps To Making Friends. Rock Hill, SC: Winthrop University.

Appendix A

Weekly Schedule

Week of	Things to Check: Tests this week Special projects due Signature needed				
Monday	Subject _____	Subject _____	Subject _____	Subject _____	Subject _____
Tuesday	Subject _____	Subject _____	Subject _____	Subject _____	Subject _____
Wednesday	Subject _____	Subject _____	Subject _____	Subject _____	Subject _____
Thursday	Subject _____	Subject _____	Subject _____	Subject _____	Subject _____
Friday	Subject _____	Subject _____	Subject _____	Subject _____	Subject _____

Keep this in your notebook and use it to write down *all* assignments each week.

Appendix B
Daily Schedule

Fill out the daily schedule with a parent. Be sure to write down scheduled activities such as sports practices, music lessons, and responsibilities like doing chores, taking a bath. Be sure to schedule in personal time for things such as playing with friends, television, and so forth. Set aside the best time for you to do your homework each day.

Monday

3:00 P.M. _____	7:00 P.M. _____
4:00 P.M. _____	8:00 P.M. _____
5:00 P.M. _____	9:00 P.M. _____
6:00 P.M. _____	10:00 P.M. _____

Tuesday

3:00 P.M. _____	7:00 P.M. _____
4:00 P.M. _____	8:00 P.M. _____
5:00 P.M. _____	9:00 P.M. _____
6:00 P.M. _____	10:00 P.M. _____

Wednesday

3:00 P.M. _____	7:00 P.M. _____
4:00 P.M. _____	8:00 P.M. _____
5:00 P.M. _____	9:00 P.M. _____
6:00 P.M. _____	10:00 P.M. _____

Thursday

3:00 P.M. _____	7:00 P.M. _____
4:00 P.M. _____	8:00 P.M. _____
5:00 P.M. _____	9:00 P.M. _____
6:00 P.M. _____	10:00 P.M. _____

Appendix C
Signs

Sign language is a useful tool in the classroom. Signs can be used by teachers to nonverbally communicate messages to students.

Come: With your index fingers out, roll your hands towards your body.

Yes: Move your fist up and down in front of you.

Quiet: Begin with your finger on your lips. Move hand down and away from the mouth.

Good: Place the tips of your fingers on your chin and move your hand out.

No: Bring your index and middle finger together in one motion to your thumb.

Stop: Chop your right hand into the palm of your left.

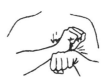

Sit Down: Both open hands are held palms down and fingers pointing forward. Move hands down a short distance.

Help: Close the left hand in the "S" sign. Lift the left hand with an open right hand.

Work: Both "S" hands are held palms down. The right hand strikes the back of the left hand several times.

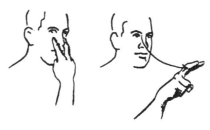

Try: Bring your index and middle finger together in one motion to your thumb.

Look: Point to your eyes, then twist your hand and point in the desired direction.

Line Up: Face palms of hands together. Move hands apart, right hand toward the chest and left outward.

Appendix D
Homework Assignments

Date _____

Reading (Yellow) _____

Spelling (Pink) _____

English (Blue) _____

Math (Green) _____

Social Studies (Orange) _____

Science/Health (Purple) _____

Other assignments or important information _____

_____

Are the assignments written down correctly? _____
Teacher's Signature

Assignments complete _____
Parent's Signature

The colors listed above represent each subject in your notebook. Color code each assignment when finished and keep it in your homework folder.

Bibliography

Frank, K.E. (1992). *Counseling Props and Metaphors: A Creative Approach to Counseling.* Rock Hill, SC: Carolina Counseling Concepts.

Smith, S.J. and Walter, G. *Four Steps To Making Friends.* Rock Hill, SC: Winthrop University.

Kim "Tip" Frank, Ed.S., LPC and Susan J. Smith, Ed.D.